KW-236-902

CONTENTS

A NOTE TO THE TEACHER

Each book in the WORKING WITH INFORMATION series has three main objectives:

1. To present information on a broad topic in language that is easily understood, with illustrations that complement the text.

2. To use the text and illustrations to give pupils practice in a wide variety of reference and study skills, including using a table of contents, using an index, using a glossary, skimming for information, note-taking, organising notes, summarising, and extracting information from graphs, tables, plans, maps and diagrams.

3. To give pupils practical experience with these skills, by providing suggestions for project work involving the finding and using of information on a topic associated with the broad theme of the book.

A general quiz on the topic is included near the end of each book. Apart from the fact that most pupils enjoy a quiz, it serves as an assessment for the teacher of the degree of assimilation that has been achieved.

Other titles in the series are:
Computers in Action
Robots at Work
Technology in the Home
Food Technology
Energy for Work

WORKING WITH INFORMATION

THE WORLD'S WEATHER

Chris Burgess

SCHOFIELD & SIMS LTD.

COMPLEMENTARY SERIES

The books in this series are complementary to the modules in STUDY READING and ENGLISH SKILLS. Together, the three series give comprehensive coverage to the skills of language communication.

WORKING WITH INFORMATION provides practice in reference and study skills, and the writing of projects.

STUDY READING is a reading development programme ranging in reading ages from 6.0 to 12.5, in which the emphasis is on the extracting of information from printed materials.

ENGLISH SKILLS deals mainly with the conventions of language usage, including as it does modules on *Punctuation*, *Written Communication*, *Spelling* and *Vocabulary*. Additionally, there are titles on *Creative Writing* and *Reference Skills*.

0 7217 0616 9
0 7217 0622 3 (Net Edition)

First printed 1987

Designed, illustrated and set by PFB Art & Type Ltd.
Printed in England by Stott Bros Ltd., Halifax

WEATHER, CLIMATE AND PEOPLE

After a long, cold winter, the first mild, sunny day of spring can bring smiles to the faces of even the gloomiest people. All our lives are affected by the weather. It dictates many of the things we do: whether to go to the beach or stay indoors and watch television.

The weather dictates the kind of clothes we wear from day to day. It makes up the farmer's mind as to which job he will do next. The work done, or not done, on a building site can be decided by the weather. Certain building jobs become impossible in pouring rain, or when the temperature falls below zero.

How much money we need to spend on vegetables and other foods can depend on the weather. Some vegetables cannot be harvested when the ground is frozen, so the price goes up. But the right amount of sun and rain can give good crops, and then food becomes cheaper.

Life and Death

Weather can be responsible for killing or seriously injuring people. Dense fog on motorways can cause fatal multi-vehicle pile-ups. Ice and snow on the roads can also cause tragedies, especially when drivers are travelling too fast or too close to other vehicles.

During very cold weather, many old people die as a result of a drop in their body temperature—they cannot keep warm. Prolonged exposure to heat can lead to heatstroke, which can result in death. In some parts of the world, hurricanes and tornadoes can bring death and destruction. A sudden thaw

The desert blooming after rain

on high mountains can set off an avalanche that wipes out a whole village. Too much rain can cause serious flooding. Years of drought can reduce people to starvation, with even those who remain alive being too weak to resist disease.

But rain after years of drought can make the desert bloom. It can bring new hope of a better life to people on the edge of despair.

All over the world, people are being affected by the weather. They are doing what they intended to do because the weather is right, or changing their plans because it is not. They are watching weather forecasts to help them with their planning. But though forecasts may help us to think ahead, they do not change the weather. We just have to make the best of it as it comes.

Weather and Climate

Weather is the condition of the air that surrounds the Earth. It may be cold or hot, clear or cloudy, calm or windy. The weather may be fine, or it may bring rain, snow, sleet or hail.

Fast-moving air may whip up the sea into high waves. Thunderstorms may burn up the air with bolts of lightning.

Lightning at the start of a thunderstorm

In some areas the weather changes from day to day, and sometimes even from hour to hour. But there are places on Earth where the weather remains the same for long periods.

Weather is the state of the air during a short period. This is not the same as climate. Climate is the average weather of an area over a long time. It is usually described in terms of the average temperatures, and the amount of rain or snow the area receives.

Every place on Earth, no matter how small, has its own climate. Places that lie far apart can have climates that are very similar. Yet there may be quite big differences between the climates of places that are close together. The climates of two villages lying near each other may have marked differences.

Even the north and south walls of the same house can have different climates!

Although Britain's weather is very variable and difficult to predict, the climate is temperate. This means that Britain is not normally subject to very high or low temperatures, such as are experienced by people living on the Earth's large land masses. Britain has what is known as a maritime climate.

Nevertheless, in Britain in February 1986, temperatures fell as low as $-14°$ Celsius. This was unusually severe weather for Britain. The average temperature in February is about $4°$ Celsius, which is mild compared with some countries. In other parts of the world, of course, some average February temperatures are higher than in Britain.

Weather Extremes

All life on Earth lives in the same thin envelope of air – the atmosphere – that surrounds our planet. But the weather that can happen in that air on the surface of the Earth can sometimes be extremely different.

The highest temperature ever recorded was $58°$ Celsius at Al Aziziyah, Libya, in September 1922, and the lowest $-88.28°$ Celsius at Vostok, Antarctica, in August 1960.

The strongest wind measured was at Mount Washington, USA, in April 1934. For five minutes it blew at 303 km/h, with one gust reaching 372 km/h.

The heaviest rainfall recorded in a day occurred in March 1952 on the island of Réunion in the Indian Ocean. In 24 hours, 186.99 centimetres fell.

The driest place on Earth is Calama, in the Atacama Desert in Chile, where rain has never been recorded.

Ice cliffs twenty-five metres high in Antarctica

AIR, WATER AND HEAT

Three things are needed before it is possible to have weather. They are air, water and heat.

Without air there would be no wind. And there would be no way of raising the water from the oceans, lakes and rivers so that it can fall again as rain, hail, sleet and snow. Without water, weather would simply be a matter of moving air, or winds.

Earth has an ample supply of water. In the atmosphere around the Earth is all the air that is needed. But without heat, everything would be still. The thing that stirs up the mixture and gets things moving is heat. The heat that is needed comes from the Sun.

One other thing that helps to keep the atmosphere in motion is the rotation of the Earth. This helps to move the air above it. Air currents all over the world are a result of a combination of heat from the Sun and the rotation of the Earth.

In a Sea of Air

The Earth's atmosphere is like a shallow sea of air surrounding the planet. The atmosphere extends upwards for about 210 kilometres, and the air gets thinner the higher you go.

It is only in the lowest eleven or so kilometres that the air is dense enough to hold water in the form of water vapour. This layer is called the troposphere, and it is the only part of the atmosphere where weather exists.

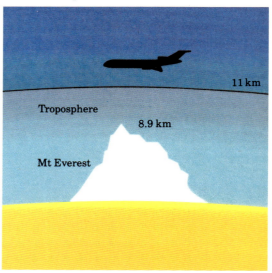

Troposphere

11 km

8.9 km

Mt Everest

Even though we cannot see air, it has weight. Pushing down on all of us, and on every part of the Earth, is the pressure of the air above. We do not notice this constant pressure because we are used to it, and our bodies are made to withstand it.

The pressure of air is not the same on all parts of the Earth. It is greatest at sea-level, and the higher you go, the less it gets. On the top of Mount Everest, the air pressure is very low.

Cold air is heavier than warmer air, so different temperatures cause differences in air pressure. A mass of cold air forms a high-pressure area. Warmer air forms a low-pressure area. The force of air pressure tends to push air from high-pressure areas to low-pressure areas.

Wind and Water

The wind is the movement of air from high-pressure areas to low-pressure areas. When there is a big difference in the pressures in the two areas, then the wind is strong.

As the air moves into a low-pressure area, it forces some of the existing air to move upwards. As this warm air moves upwards, it grows cooler. Cold air cannot hold as much water vapour as warm air can, so the water vapour in the rising air condenses—that is, it changes from vapour into tiny drops of water.

These droplets do not fall to Earth. They are held aloft by the current of rising air. A cloud is formed when millions of these drops of water come together. This is why low-pressure areas are usually cloudy.

Clouds

The air moving out of a high-pressure area moves near the ground. As it moves away to the low-pressure area, it is replaced by air from above. This sinking air grows warmer, and is then able to hold more moisture. It is able to evaporate any clouds in the area. That is why high-pressure areas are usually clear, giving fine weather.

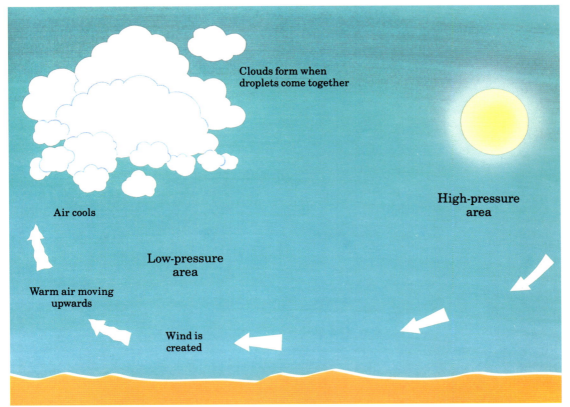

Clouds form when droplets come together

High-pressure area

Air cools

Low-pressure area

Warm air moving upwards

Wind is created

Winter fog in Richmond Park

Fog and Precipitation

Moisture enters the atmosphere as water vapour. Water vapour cannot be seen, but it is there all the same. The amount of water vapour in the air is known as the humidity of the air. When air is very humid, it means that there is a great deal of moisture in it. Air that feels very dry is low in humidity.

There comes a point when air cannot hold any more water vapour. It is then said to be saturated. When the temperature of saturated air begins to fall, the air cannot go on holding the water vapour. The moisture condenses into droplets of water, forming clouds.

If this happens near to the ground, low clouds called fog may develop.

When the droplets of water combine and become too heavy to remain in the air, they fall to the ground. This is rain, which is one form of precipitation. Other forms of precipitation are snow, sleet and hail.

Snow or sleet is formed when the air near the ground is at or near freezing. Hail can develop when ice crystals move up and down between the top and bottom layers of a thundercloud. As they travel, the ice crystals go on getting bigger, until finally they fall to Earth as hailstones.

Rain in London

Mist hanging in a valley on a cool morning will disperse as the Sun warms the air

AIR, WATER AND HEAT

THE GREAT WEATHER ENGINES

The beach at Bridlington, Yorkshire

If you have stayed at the seaside in fine weather, you may have noticed that a breeze often springs up in the afternoon. It blows from the sea to the land.

Land warms up in sunshine much more quickly than water does. As the land heats up during the day, so does the air above it. But the air above the sea remains cooler. The air pressure on the land becomes lower than the air pressure on the sea. So the air moves from the sea to the land. This is the afternoon sea breeze.

This is reversed during the night. The land cools quicker than the sea. The air pressure on the sea becomes lower than that on the land. So the cooler air from the land moves on to the sea. This is the night-time land breeze.

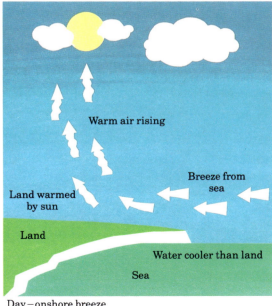

Day – onshore breeze

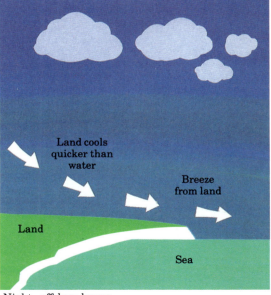

Night – offshore breeze

Continents and Oceans

What we notice happening at the seaside, happens on a much bigger scale on the continents and oceans of the world. During the long summer days, the large continents become very warm. But the temperature of the oceans around them changes very little. So in summer, the warm air over the continents rises, and the cooler, moist air from the oceans moves in to take its place.

This cooler air is heated by the warm land, and it in turn rises above the continent. As the air rises it cools, and the water vapour in it turns to cloud, which in turn gives heavy rain. The rain is usually heaviest near the edges of the land, because the air dries out as it moves deeper into the continent.

The opposite happens in winter. The land cools down, and the cooling air above it flows out to sea. With no moisture coming from the sea, there is less cloud and the skies are clear. This results in long periods of very cold, clear weather, between shorter periods of snow. In these conditions, snow remains on the ground throughout the winter and does not melt until the spring.

Kicking Horse Pass, Canada, on a typical cold day in winter

This constant movement of air over continents and oceans is one of the great weather engines that control the climates of the world.

Poles and Equator

Another weather engine that moves huge masses of air about is the wide range of temperatures between the North and South Poles and the equator.

Air near the equator becomes very hot, and it rises. This leaves an area of low pressure, and the surrounding air rushes in to fill it. At the North and South Poles, the opposite is happening. The air at the Poles is very cold and heavy, so it sinks down, creating an area of high pressure.

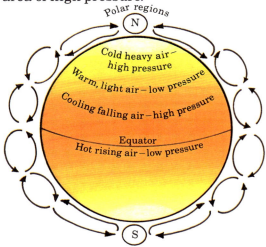

Polar regions

N

Cold heavy air – high pressure

Warm, light air – low pressure

Cooling falling air – high pressure

Equator
Hot rising air – low pressure

S

The pressure zones lie around the Earth in bands like this – but this diagram is very simplified

The rising air at the equator spreads out both north and south, and as it does so it cools and becomes heavy. It then sinks back to Earth between the equator and the poles, making areas of high pressure.

Air is constantly on the move between these areas of different pressures. This movement is like a great engine that never stops. As are all the weather engines of the world, it is powered by the heat of the Sun.

The Spinning Earth

If the Earth was all land or all sea, the winds of the world would be steady systems, and weather forecasting would be easy. But it is much more complicated than that. To begin with, the huge land masses are not spread evenly round the world. Also, moving air behaves very differently over flat, low land and over high mountain ranges.

Another complication is that the Earth is not still: it is spinning all the time. Without this spin, it is probable that the winds between the equator and the poles would travel directly north and south.

The effect of the Earth rotating is to curve the movements of the winds, so that in some parts of the world they tend to move more westerly or easterly — all of which makes weather forecasting a very complicated business.

The Earth from space, showing the whirls of cloud caused by winds

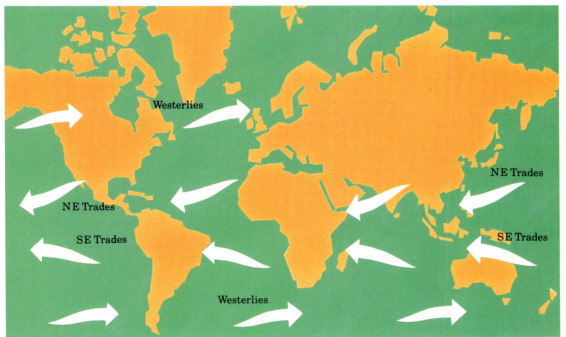

Trends of the Earth's winds

THE GREAT WEATHER ENGINES

4 BATTLES IN THE ATMOSPHERE

The story of weather is really a tale of battles in the atmosphere, between huge masses of air, rising and falling, and advancing and retreating. The results of these battles give us our weather.

In a temperate country such as Britain, it is not unusual to have a warm, wet day followed by a cold, dry day. What has happened? Has the air altered in some way?

All that has happened is that yesterday's air has moved on. The warm, moist air of yesterday has been pushed away by air that is cold and dry. This sudden change of weather is just a small skirmish in the world-wide struggle between warm and cold air.

The Big Build-up

The huge air masses that take part in this conflict build up in places where the air is very slow-moving for a long period. An air mass building up over a hot, dry desert is itself hot and dry. An air mass forming over the frozen Arctic Ocean is wet and cold. Such air masses

can cover an area of thirteen million square kilometres—about fifty times the size of Britain.

Once an air mass begins to move, two things start to happen. It can bring changes of weather to the areas over which it passes, and the air mass can itself begin to change. For example, a warm air mass moving over cold ground will cool down at the bottom.

Any area that lies well within the main body of an air mass usually has settled weather. The areas where weather changes occur are where air masses meet. These areas are called fronts. The battles between warm and cold air take place along these fronts.

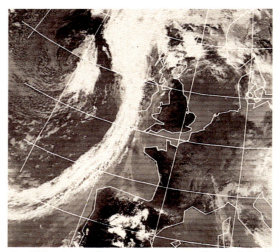

A cold front, seen from space as a curved band of cloud, approaching Britain from the Atlantic Ocean

Warm and Cold Fronts

Warm air is lighter than cold air, and they do not normally mix. Warm air always tends to rise above colder air.

When warm air masses and cold air masses meet, the one which is moving faster pushes the other out of the way.

A warm front

When the warm air is moving faster, it runs up the side of the colder air, and pushes it away. This is called a warm front. But if the cold air is travelling faster, it burrows under the warmer air. This forms a cold front.

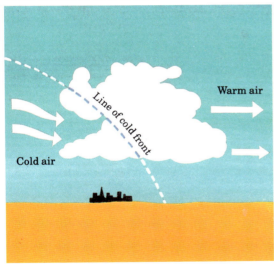

A cold front

The world north of the equator is called the Northern Hemisphere. The Southern Hemisphere is south of the equator. The cold air from the poles is separated from the warmer air coming from the equator by polar fronts. These are the areas where they meet.

Weather in the region of a polar front is often very unsettled, with changes taking place from day to day. The British Isles lie in the region of the northern polar front, and that is why it is difficult to say what British weather will do next. Along a polar front, the warm and cold air are continually battling it out.

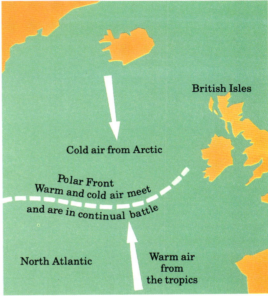

The North Atlantic polar front

Depressions

Each polar front lies in an east-west direction round the world. On either side of the front, the air flows in opposite directions. Sometimes the warm air from the south edges into the colder air from the north. This makes a bump in the front. This disturbance creates a wave of air that grows bigger as it travels eastward along the polar front.

At the crest of the wave, an area of low pressure forms and winds begin to blow round it. The two sides of the bump try to move together and in so doing they create what is called a depression.

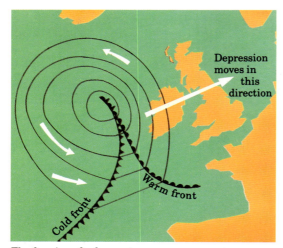
The forming of a depression

A depression is an area of low pressure, with the air spiralling round it. In a deep depression, where the pressure is very low, the spiralling wind can whip up to gale force.

Although these winds can be very strong on and near the British Isles, they do not compare in force with the depressions that occur in some parts of the world. One of the worst storms, the hurricane, happens in many parts of the world. Wind speeds in a hurricane can exceed 200 km/h.

In different places, the hurricane has different names. In Australia it is known as a willy-willy, and in Asia it is called a typhoon or cyclone. Some of these storms are so violent that they can devastate stretches of land for hundreds of kilometres. They blow down houses, hurl cars through the air, and create huge waves that destroy shipping and even break up concrete harbours.

Damage left by a hurricane

A hurricane seen from space

BATTLES IN THE ATMOSPHERE

The centre of a hurricane seen from ground level

Hurricanes measure many kilometres across. A very narrow depression, which can be measured in metres, is the tornado. This usually starts over land, and the wind speed has been estimated at well over 480 km/h. A tornado that starts over the sea is called a waterspout.

A giant waterspout

4

BATTLES IN THE ATMOSPHERE

WEATHER INFORMATION WORLD-WIDE

Accurate weather forecasts depend on a knowledge of weather conditions throughout the world. Fortunately, the nations work closely together in helping each other to gather this information. More than 140 countries belong to the World Weather Watch programme. Information collected by each country is distributed to all members.

A weather station on Aldabra, an island in the Indian Ocean

Observations

Around the world there are about 3500 observation stations. Hourly measurements are made of temperature, air pressure, wind speed and direction, rainfall, humidity, and other weather conditions. All this information is transmitted to centres where weather forecasts are prepared.

A weather-vane

A meteorologist taking weather measurements

Observation stations are equipped with a variety of instruments. Thermometers measure air temperature. Weather-vanes show wind direction. Anemometers measure the speed of the wind. Barometers show air pressure. Humidity is indicated by hygrometers. The amount of rainfall or snowfall is measured by rain gauges.

An anemometer tower—alongside is a cloud searchlight

In some stations, radar is used to detect rain falling in distant areas. Radio waves are sent out, and are reflected back to the station by raindrops and ice particles in the clouds. The rainy area appears on a screen like a television.

Radar helps meteorologists to assess the speed and direction of a storm. The strength of the reflected radio waves shows the type of storm that is approaching. All this information helps the meteorologist to work out when a storm will reach a certain area.

Besides land-based stations, facilities for observations include weather-ships, satellites, aircraft, balloons, and even special ocean buoys that record weather conditions at sea level. They transmit their information to meteorological stations based on land.

Weather Balloons

About 1600 weather balloons are launched around the world every day. The balloons are filled with a lighter-than-air gas, such as helium or hydrogen. They carry an instrument called a radiosonde, a miniature radio transmitter, which sends information back to Earth.

A radiosonde balloon being sent up

A constant-level weather balloon ready to be raised

Direction-finding equipment is used to track the movement of the balloons, from which the speed and direction of the wind can be traced. The gas inside the balloon expands as it rises. At about 27 000 metres, the balloon bursts. The radiosonde is then carried back to Earth by parachute.

Another item of equipment is the constant-level balloon. It floats at a certain altitude for many months, and provides long-term measurements of weather conditions at that level. The information is transmitted to satellites, which then relay it to ground stations.

Satellites

Artificial satellites are sent into Earth orbit by rockets. Some of them carry television cameras that show the pattern of clouds above the Earth, and regions of snow and ice on the surface. Signals carrying pictures are beamed from satellites to receiving stations on Earth, where photographs are prepared from the signals.

A satellite photograph showing the British Isles through a window in cloud

These photographs can show dangerous storms developing over the oceans. Meteorologists can then issue warnings before the storms hit the land.

One kind of satellite is called polar-orbiting. It circles the Earth at an altitude of between 800 and 1400 kilometres. During each orbit, it travels over the North and South Poles. As the Earth is rotating all the time, the satellite travels over different parts of the Earth during each orbit. Some polar-orbiting satellites can photograph the entire Earth twice each day.

A Landsat weather satellite in orbit

Another kind of satellite is the geostationary satellite. It is stationed over the Earth's equator at an altitude of about 36 000 kilometres. As the satellite moves at the same speed as the rotation of the Earth, it remains in the same position over the Earth all the time.

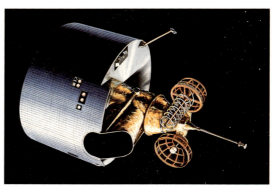

A geostationary satellite

Because of their high orbit, geostationary satellites can photograph much wider areas of the Earth than polar-orbiting satellites. Four properly-placed geostationary satellites can cover the entire Earth at once.

HERE IS THE WEATHER FORECAST

Weather maps, such as those we see on television, are made from the information collected from all over the world. Some of the maps show the weather as it is at present, while others show what the weather is likely to be in the near future.

Isobars and Fronts

The weather maps seen on television and in the newspapers are maps that show conditions just above the Earth's surface. Most of them have lines called isobars. These lines connect places that have the same air pressure. Winds are inclined to blow almost parallel to these isobars. In places where the isobars are close together, the winds are strong. When the isobars are far apart, the winds are much weaker.

Also on the maps, the positions of warm, cold and stationary fronts are shown by the use of symbols. It is in the area of warm and cold fronts that the weather is most likely to be unsettled.

Other symbols are used to show features such as temperature, wind speed and direction, and areas of rain, snow and sunshine.

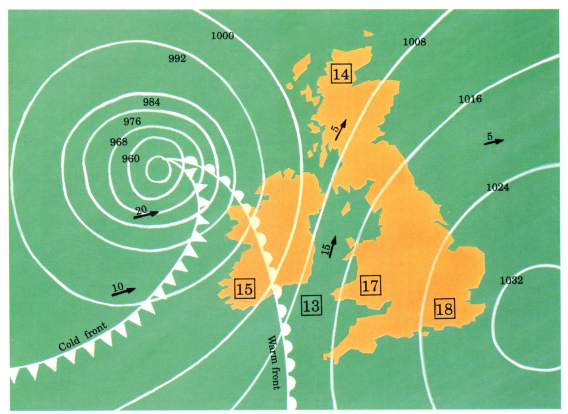

A weather map similar to the ones usually seen in the newspapers

Making a Forecast

A meteorologist may examine a number of weather maps before making a forecast. The maps can show only what the weather is like now, and what it has been like. How can the meteorologist decide what the weather is going to be like?

Looking at the isobars and fronts on a weather map is a good beginning. These change as they move, but usually they change only gradually. Very roughly, the meteorologist finds out which way the weather is moving. It is then a matter of predicting where the isobars and fronts will move to in a certain time.

For example, round the British Isles we know that the weather usually moves roughly from west to east. So, if the weather map shows a warm front moving into Ireland from the Atlantic, it is fairly certain that it will soon be felt in Britain.

Weather forecasters at work

Wrong Forecasts

Weather forecasts are not always correct, despite the use of expensive equipment, including computers. The formulas used by computers are only approximate descriptions of the ways in which weather can behave. Also, there are so many possible weather conditions, and these conditions can change very quickly for various reasons. Forecast maps are much more accurate in predicting the general condition of the atmosphere than in predicting the weather in a particular place at a certain time.

Another reason for poor forecasts is that not enough weather observations are made throughout the world. Most land areas are well served, but there are too few weather-ships, aircraft and ocean buoys to cover the oceans. This is because the oceans cover more than two-thirds of the Earth's surface. Over large areas of the ocean, the weather is rarely observed except by satellites. Acting alone, satellites do not give all the information that is required for accurate forecasting.

The Future

Meteorology is a science that is changing very rapidly. Satellites, for example, are opening up new possibilities in weather forecasting. Acting alone, satellites do not give all the information that is required for accurate forecasting, but they may help to overcome the difficulties of having too few observation stations in some parts of the world.

It is likely that there will be an increase in the number of automatic weather-stations. These could be triggered into action by a weather satellite as it passes overhead. The satellite could then pick up weather information from the station and transmit it to weather centres.

The increased use of computers will also help. They can analyse masses of information much quicker than people can. In the future, it is possible that a satellite with a built-in computer will process information as it receives it, and send weather centres a forecast for the area over which it is passing.

And probably you will be able to tune in to the weather satellite on your television set at any time of the day or night.

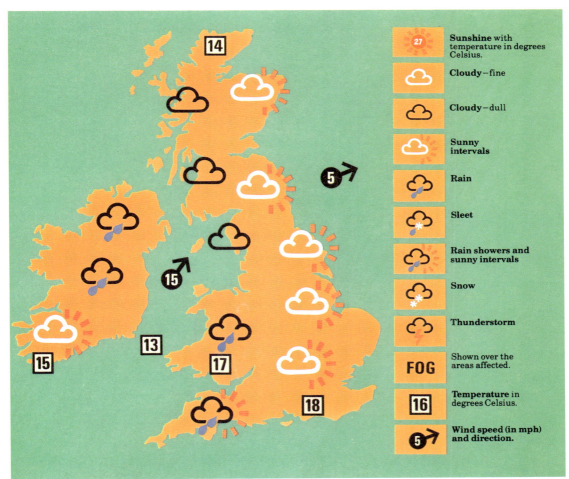

A weather map similar to the ones shown on television

GLOSSARY

artificial satellite
a man-made object launched into orbit round a planet

atmosphere
the envelope of air that surrounds the Earth

buoy
a floating marker

climate
the general pattern of weather conditions of a place over a long period of time

depression
the centre of an area of low air pressure

equator
an imaginary circle round the Earth, midway between the North and South Poles

front
the region between two masses of air of different temperatures

geostationary satellite
a satellite in stationary orbit over the equator

hemisphere
half of a sphere, or half of the Earth

humidity
the amount of water vapour in the air

isobar
a line on a map passing through places where atmospheric pressure is the same

meteorology
the study of weather and climate

polar-orbiting satellite
a satellite that orbits the Earth via the North and South Poles

precipitation
a fall of rain, snow, sleet or hail

radar
a method of finding the position of an object by means of radio-wave echoes

radiosonde
a miniature radio transmitter that sends weather information back to Earth, usually from a balloon

symbol
a sign or mark that stands for something else

temperate country
a country that does not have extremely hot or cold weather

troposphere
a layer of atmosphere extending about 11 kilometres upwards from the Earth's surface, in which temperature falls with height

vapour
moisture in the air

weather
the state of the atmosphere at any one time

REFERENCE AND STUDY SKILLS PRACTICE

1. Use the list of Contents on page 3 to answer the questions.

In which chapter in this book are you likely to find the following information? Answer by giving the Chapter number or numbers, and the Chapter title or titles.

(a) How weather centres gather information.

(b) The difference between weather and climate.

(c) How weather is affected by heat from the Sun.

(d) Why weather forecasts are not always accurate.

2. The answer to each question is somewhere in this book. In each question, dark type is used to show the key word or words. Find the key word or words in the Index at the end of the book. Beside the entry in the Index is a page number or numbers. Somewhere on that page or pages you will find the information you need. Use the information you find to answer the questions as briefly as possible.

(a) In what way are **buoys** used in meteorology?

(b) What other names are given to **hurricanes** in some parts of the world?

(c) What is **fog**, and how does it develop?

(d) How might an **automatic weather-station** operate?

3. Use the Index to help you find the answers. First, decide which is the key word or words in each sentence. Then continue as in Question 2.

(a) What gives air humidity?

(b) Why is helium sometimes used in weather balloons?

(c) What is the purpose of a hygrometer?

(d) Give one advantage of using computers in meteorology.

4. Use the Glossary to help you find the answers.

(a) What are the differences between geostationary satellites and polar-orbiting satellites?

(b) What facts does a meteorologist need before it is possible to draw an isobar?

(c) Is the troposphere part of the atmosphere?

(d) Name the different kinds of precipitation.

5. When you are working on a project, it may be useful to make a brief summary of a part of the book you are using. Here is a brief summary of the section 'Poles and Equator', which begins on page 12. Read that section, and then read the summary below.

The differences in temperature at the poles and the equator move masses of air. Hot air rises from the equator, leaving low pressure, into which the surrounding air rushes.

Cold, heavy air from the poles sinks down, creating high pressure. As air from the equator spreads north and south, it cools and sinks back to Earth between the equator and the poles, making areas of high pressure.

Air is moved constantly by this great engine which is powered by heat from the Sun.

The original passage of 160 words has been summarised in 83 words.

(a) The passage beginning on page 14, 'Warm and Cold Fronts', contains 195 words. Write a summary of the passage in not more than 110 words.

(b) The passage beginning on page 19, 'Weather Balloons', contains 135 words. Write a summary of the passage in not more than 65 words.

6. Project work often involves you in making very brief notes from a book. These notes remind you of facts that you might wish to include in your work. Notes need not be written down as sentences. They are simply reminders, and should be as brief as possible. Here is a set of notes on the passage 'In a Sea of Air', on page 8.

Atmosphere like shallow sea−extends about 210 km−air thinner with height−only bottom 11 km (troposphere) holds water vapour−where weather exists−air has weight which presses down−our bodies made to withstand−air pressure greatest at sea-level−pressure decreases with height−cold air heavier than warm−temperature affects pressure−mass of cold air gives high pressure−warm air gives low pressure−air moves from high-pressure to low-pressure areas.

(a) Make a set of notes on the passage headed 'Wind and Water', which begins on page 9.

(b) Make a set of notes on the passage headed 'Depressions', which begins on page 15.

REFERENCE AND STUDY SKILLS PRACTICE

7. Skimming is a quick way of finding what you want from a page of print. Let your eyes run quickly from left to right, and from the top to the bottom of the page. Do not try to read every word. When you think you have found what you are looking for, stop and read it carefully. Make sure it is what you want. The more you practise skimming, the faster you get.

Use skimming to find answers to these questions. The number of the page on which you will find the answer is in brackets after the question.

(a) What is the purpose of an anemometer? (18)
(b) What is the heaviest recorded rainfall, and where did it occur? (7)
(c) What happens to water vapour when it condenses? (9)
(d) How do hailstones develop? (10)
(e) During the night-time, why does a breeze usually blow from the land on to the sea? (11)

8. Here is a set of notes taken from 'Fog and Precipitation' in Chapter 2, but the notes are in the wrong order. Write the notes in their correct order.

low temperature makes water vapour in saturated air condense — precipitation: rain, snow, sleet, hail — high humidity means much water vapour — fall as hailstones — changes to droplets of water — snow or sleet when air near ground certain temperature — unseen moisture in air is water vapour — if near ground, fog may develop — hail developed by up and down movement of ice crystals between top and bottom of thundercloud — combining droplets give rain — water vapour gives air humidity — low humidity means little vapour

9. Answer the questions by looking at the weather forecast maps on pages 21 and 23.

(a) Where is the main area of low pressure?
(b) What is the weather likely to be in the Atlantic Ocean just west of Ireland?
(c) What wind speeds are forecast in the Irish Sea?
(d) What is the forecast for the temperature in the south of England?
(e) What is the direction of the wind in the north of Scotland?

PROJECTS

This book gives you some information on the world's weather. But there is still a great deal more you can learn, and a good way to do so is to find out as much as you can about one aspect of weather, and write up the information as a project.

On page 29 is a list of suggested topics. First, choose one that interests you, and then go to work on it. You may find some of the information you need in this book, but you will also have to use encyclopedias and other books of information.

Project work is much easier to manage when you go about it in an organised way. Take it one step at a time, like this:

Step One

Choose a topic that interests you. If you cannot find one in the list, think of one yourself.

Step Two

Make a start by finding a few books that may contain the information you need. If you use an encyclopedia, look up 'weather' in the Index. There may be sub-headings that will be of use to you. Decide how many sections or chapters you need for your topic, and write a title or heading for each one.

Step Three

Find the details you need. As you find the information, make notes. The notes may be in any order. At this stage the main thing is to make plenty of them.

Step Four

Organise your notes. This means rearranging the notes in the sections or chapters to which they belong. When you have done this, you may find that you have plenty of notes for some chapters, and not enough for others. And you may decide to get rid of some chapters and create new ones. So you have to find some more information before you are fully organised.

Step Five

Write your first draft. Use your notes and write out the project chapter by chapter. At this stage get it all down quickly. It is called the first draft because it will need correcting and rewriting.

Step Six

Write your fair copy. This is the final product, so make it look good and easy to read. Check spellings about which you are doubtful. Take care with your punctuation. Include illustrations. As you go along, improve on your first draft in any way you can.

SUGGESTIONS FOR TOPICS

The Climate of the British Isles

The Monsoon Season in India

Hurricanes and Tornadoes

The Work of the Meteorologist

Instruments That Measure Weather

Transport and Weather

Weather and the Farmer

Clothes and Climate

Thunderstorms

Controlling the Weather

PROJECTS

QUIZ

1. Which three things are necessary to make weather?

2. How many geostationary satellites are required to give coverage of the whole Earth?

3. What do we call the average weather of an area over a long period?

4. Why are polar-orbiting satellites so called?

5. What do we call a very long period without rain?

6. What is needed to change water into water vapour?

7. What is condensation?

8. Why is there no weather 500 kilometres above the Earth?

9. Why do the winds at the polar front not move directly north and south?

10. Why do we not feel the pressure of the air above us?

11. Does air move from a low-pressure area to a high-pressure area?

12. Which is the heavier — warm air or cold air?

13. Why does air moving out of a high-pressure area move near the ground?

14. What kind of weather is usually found in high-pressure areas?

15. In which parts of the world are there not enough observations of weather?

16. What is a sea breeze, and when and how does it develop?

17. What is the source of power for the weather engines of the world?

18. What is a weather front?

19. When a warm air mass and a cold air mass meet, which one is usually pushed out of the way?

20. What is the name of the instrument that measures air pressure?

INDEX

ACKNOWLEDGEMENTS

The author and the publishers wish to thank the following for permission to use copyright material:

Science Photo Library: pp. 6 (Dr. Peter Moore), 7 (Doug Allan), 17 (J. G. Golden)

P. P. H. Hattinga Verschure, Deventer, Netherlands: p. 6 (centre)

Art Directors Photo Library: pp. 8, 10 (3), 11, 12, 17 (left), 18 (left, foot)

J. F. P. Galvin: pp. 9, 18 (top)

Space Frontiers/Daily Telegraph Colour Library: pp. 13, 20 (3)

University of Dundee: p. 14

Daily Telegraph Colour Library: p. 16

NASA/Daily Telegraph Colour Library: p. 16 (foot)

Geoffrey C. M. Taylor (meteorological observer): p. 18 (left, top)

J. E. L. Hulbert: p. 18 (right, foot)

Controller of Her Majesty's Stationery Office: pp. 19 (top), 22 (Crown copyright)

B. J. Burton: p. 19